KENYA

An Imprint of Scholastic Library Publishing
Danbury, Connecticut

Published for Grolier,
an imprint of Scholastic Library Publishing
Old Sherman Turnpike, Danbury, Connecticut 06816
by Times Editions,
an imprint of Times Media Pte Ltd

Copyright © 2004 Times Media Pte Ltd, Singapore
First Grolier Printing 2004

Set ISBN: 0-7172-5788-6
Volume ISBN: 0-7172-5795-9

Library of Congress Cataloging-in-Publication Data
Kenya.
p. cm.—(Fiesta!)
Summary: Discusses the festivals and holidays of Kenya and how the songs, food,
and traditions associated with these celebrations reflect the culture of the people.
1. Festivals—Kenya—Juvenile literature. 2. Kenya—Social life and customs—Juvenile literature.
[1. Festivals—Kenya. 2. Holidays—Kenya. 3. Kenya—Social life and customs.]
I. Grolier (Firm). II. Fiesta! (Danbury, Conn.)
GT4889.K4K45   2004
394.266762—dc21   2003044849

For this volume
Author: Nuala Ribeiro-Alibhai & Paul A. Rozario
Editor: Balvinder Sandhu
Designer: Benson Tan
Production: Nor Sidah Haron
Crafts and Recipes produced by Stephen Russell

Printed in Malaysia

Adult supervision advised for all crafts and recipes,
particularly those involving sharp instruments and heat.

CONTENTS

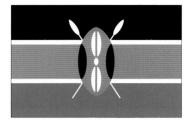

KENYA:

Located in East Africa, Kenya is bordered by Ethiopia to the north, Somalia to the northeast, Tanzania to the south, and Uganda to the west. The Indian Ocean lies to the east of Kenya. Nairobi is its capital city.

SUDAN

UGANDA

Maralal

Kisumu

Nakuru

Lake Victoria

Maasai Mara

TANZANIA

◄ Africa's largest lake, **Lake Victoria,** has shores on three countries — Kenya, Uganda, and Tanzania. Fishing and boating are the most important economic activities here. John Speke was the first European to see the lake in 1858, and he named it for Britain's Queen Victoria.

◄ **Mombasa** is the second largest city in Kenya. It enjoys a tropical climate and has the largest port on the coast of East Africa. Mombasa is a famous tourist area because of its beautiful beaches and clear waters. It was an important port for voyagers and traders from Arabia, Portugal, India, the Far East, and England.

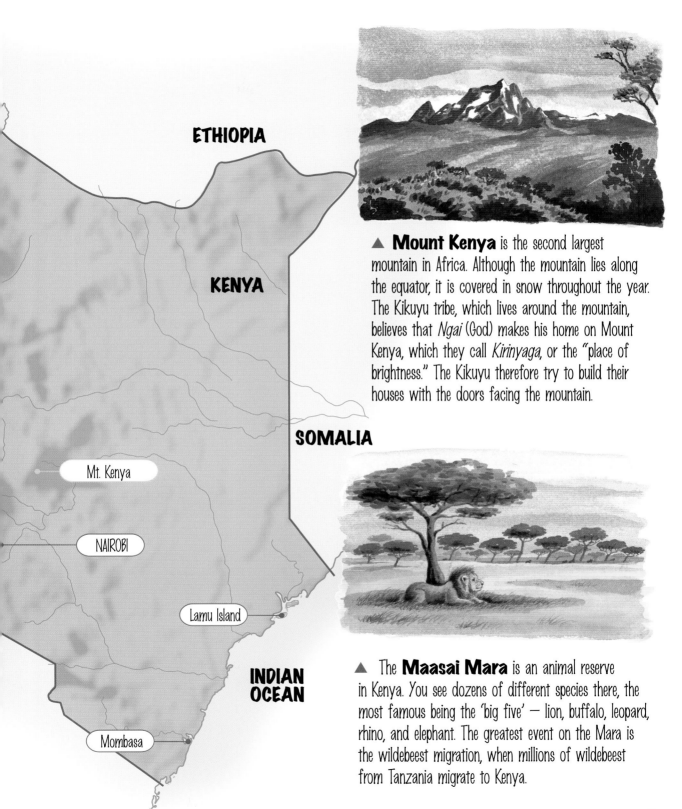

ETHIOPIA

KENYA

SOMALIA

Mt. Kenya

NAIROBI

Lamu Island

INDIAN
OCEAN

Mombasa

▲ **Mount Kenya** is the second largest mountain in Africa. Although the mountain lies along the equator, it is covered in snow throughout the year. The Kikuyu tribe, which lives around the mountain, believes that *Ngai* (God) makes his home on Mount Kenya, which they call *Kirinyaga*, or the "place of brightness." The Kikuyu therefore try to build their houses with the doors facing the mountain.

▲ The **Maasai Mara** is an animal reserve in Kenya. You see dozens of different species there, the most famous being the 'big five' — lion, buffalo, leopard, rhino, and elephant. The greatest event on the Mara is the wildebeest migration, when millions of wildebeest from Tanzania migrate to Kenya.

RELIGIONS

The main religions of Kenya are Christianity, Islam, and African traditional religions. There are also several other religions that are followed by the country's smaller communities.

THERE are three main religions in Kenya: Christianity, African traditional religions, and Islam. There is also a small community of Asian Indians, who are Hindus.

Christian Kenyans are either Catholic or Protestant. Thirty-eight percent of Kenyans are Protestants, while 28 percent of them are Roman Catholics. Kenya's Protestants are divided into different groups, including Anglican, Lutheran, Presbyterian, and Evangelical churches. Easter and Christmas are the major Christian celebrations.

Most of Kenya's Christians live in central and western Kenya. The Muslims are concentrated in eastern Kenya, particularly on the Indian Ocean coast, where there is a lot of Arabic influence. About 6 percent of Kenya's population is Muslim, and their main festivals are Id-ul-Fitr and Maulidi.

Many Kenyans practice some forms of traditional African religions. They are often animistic in nature. This means that followers believe that spirits inhabit all natural objects, including rivers, rocks, and trees. Many of Kenya's ethnic groups, such as the Maasai and Samburu, practice animistic religions.

Over the years Kenyans have mixed some traditional

One of the main characters in Christianity is the angel Gabriel.

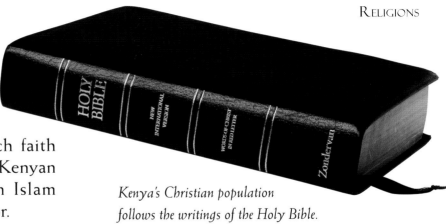

African customs with either Christianity or Islam, depending on which faith they follow. This has led to Kenyan Christianity and Kenyan Islam having a truly African flavor.

Kenya's Christian population follows the writings of the Holy Bible.

GREETINGS FROM **KENYA!**

Kenya is a diverse country made up of many different ethnic groups, including the Kikuyu, Luhiya, Luo, Kalenjin, Kamba, Kisii, and Meru. Each ethnic group has its own language. However, the national languages of Kenya are English and Kiswahili, an African language that is also spoken by people in Tanzania and Uganda.

How do you say...

Hello
Jambo

Welcome
Karibu

How are you?
Habari?

Goodbye!
Kwaheri

Thank you
Asante

Id-ul-Fitr

The most important festival for Kenyan Muslims is Id-ul-Fitr (Festival of Breaking the Fast). It is celebrated at the end of the Muslim fasting month of Ramadan.

Muslim prayer mats are often elaborately decorated.

On Id-ul-Fitr Muslims come together to offer prayers and exchange greetings. It is also a time for visiting loved ones.

Muslims get out of bed before sunrise, take a bath, wear new or clean clothes, eat dates, and set out for the mosque. Before the prayers begin, there is a cleansing ritual of washing the hands and feet.

It is only the male members of the family that go to the mosque.

A special prayer called *Namaz* is often said at this time. However, it can be done anytime between sunrise and afternoon.

The *imam* (priest) recites the *namaz* in a loud, clear voice, and it echoes across the prayer hall. A charitable gift called *sadaka fitr* is given to the poor.

When the *namaz* is over, Muslims greets each other with *"Id Mubarak"* or *"Happy Id"* and embrace three times. Muslims visit friends and neighbors, bringing a cake or other sweet dish as a gift. It is a tradition for adults to put some money in the palms of children's hands as they greet them.

A goat is slaughtered according to the customs of Islam. This meat is not consumed by the family but given to the poor. The main meal is held in the afternoon, and the dish served is *biryani*, or spiced rice cooked with meat.

Chicken biryani, *a delicious dish of spiced rice cooked with chicken.*

MAANDAZI (SWAHILI DOUGHNUTS)

YOU WILL NEED
1 cup flour
1 ¼ teaspoons baking powder
2 tablespoons sugar
Pinch of salt
1 egg
¼ cup coconut milk
A few cardamom pods with seeds removed and crushed

1 Sift the flour and baking powder.

2 Add sugar, salt, and crushed cardamom.

3 In a separate bowl beat the egg well, and add coconut milk.

4 Stir the egg mixture into the flour, and mix until a soft dough is formed. Add some water if necessary.

5 Knead the dough until it is smooth but not sticky. The dough should leave the sides of the bowl cleanly.

6 Cover with a towel, and let the dough rise in a warm place for 30 minutes.

7 Roll out the dough on a floured board until about an inch thick.

8 Cut into triangles. Deep fry in oil until golden brown. Drain on paper towels.

In the evening families join in the celebrations at a fun-fair. A special milkshake called *faluda* is drunk.

The event is held in the central park, and the whole evening is spent there. Children enjoy the rides while parents spend time chatting with friends. Children love the cotton candy, chips, and *mushkaki* (skewered roasted meat) that are served.

9

CHRISTMAS

Christians all over Kenya celebrate Christmas. It remembers the birth of Jesus Christ and is a time of great joy. On this day families travel long distances to be together to offer prayers and exchange greetings.

On Christmas Eve groups of people in choirs go singing from house to house. Each home-owner gives them a gift, which is usually money. On Christmas day the singers present whatever they collected to the church.

Most families attend church on Christmas morning, and everyone, especially children, wears new clothes bought for the occasion. It is common to see children in garments with African prints.

In a Roman Catholic church service there is a lot of singing, dancing, and clapping. The music is often based on traditional English Christmas hymns and carols, which are translated into Kiswahili. Musical instruments such as drums and shakers are played to accompany the singing.

The church is nicely decorated with flowers, ribbons, tinsel, garlands, tropical green plants, and Christmas trees.

Jesus was born in a stable in Bethlehem, and this scene is recreated in a créche, or crib. The crib is found in a corner of the church and features small statues of the infant Jesus, his mother Mary, Joseph, the shepherds, and three Magi, or wise men.

The Christmas meal is usually served in nicely designed plates and bowls, such as the one below.

An enormous star made with a wooden frame and crepe paper hangs outside the church. This star symbolizes the Star of Bethlehem, which guided the Magi to Jesus's manger. After the service families visit friends and relatives. Sometimes families also visit the sick and poor and take along with them a gift of a Christmas cake.

The main meal is eaten in the late afternoon. Great amounts of food are prepared, including *nyama choma*, which is roasted meat, usually of goat or beef. It is accompanied by *chapati* (a fresh-baked African flatbread similar to the Indian version).

People living in the cities have a special cream Christmas cake. European and Indian Christian families have a meal of pork, ham, or turkey, similar to the Christmas dinners eaten in Europe and the United States.

Items with the image of the baby Jesus, his mother Mary, and Joesph can be seen during Christmas .

USIKU MKUU (SILENT NIGHT)

Usiku mkuu!   Mtakatifu!   Uko Utulivu

Bikira   amezaa   Mwana

Mtoto   Mtakatifu   in Bwana

Alale   amanini,   Alale   amanini

MIGRATION ON THE MARA

The Maasai call the grassy plains of southern Kenya and northern Tanzania the Mara. It is on the Mara that a spectacular festival of animals takes place each year during the annual wildebeest migration.

The Mara is home to many animals such as antelopes, zebras, lions, leopards, and elephants.

The wildebeest is a kind of antelope that looks like a cross between a cow and a horse. It has a large head, horns, a mane, and a hump. It can run very fast when it wants to.

Animal conservationists believe that there are up to 1.4 million wildebeest in Kenya and Tanzania, and many of them go on the migration. Other animals such as the zebra and gazelle, another kind of antelope, also move with the wildebeest. And of course, there are the big cats, such as lions and leopards, which follow the wildebeest in the hope of being able to feed on this moving feast!

The migration begins on the Serengeti Plain in northern Tanzania early in the year. The wildebeest and zebra gather there to feed on the rich grass. The

The famous "big five" of Africa (right) are the elephant, lion, rhinoceros, leopard, and buffalo.

wildebeest also give birth to their calves, and that increases the numbers of animals that will migrate.

By April most of the grass on the Serengeti has been eaten up, and the herds begin moving north in search of new grass. This coincides with the period of the long rains, and much of the Mara in Kenya is full of lush grass.

By this time the herds have gotten larger, until there are over a million wildebeest moving into southern Kenya. Many visitors from all over the world, especially wildlife photographers, visit the Mara to experience and record this great wildlife drama.

By July the animals have reached the Mara River, which they must cross before they can finally reach the fresh pastures on the other side. This river crossing is a dangerous obstacle the wildebeest have to face.

The river is swift and deep because of the heavy rains. There are also crocodiles in the river that will eat the animals that take too long to swim across to the other side.

Many of the younger wildebeest are swept away by the river currents or eaten by crocodiles. But most of them make it across the river and spend the next three months in the Kenyan part of the Mara, feasting on grass. Later in the year they return south to Tanzania, where they will start the migration again the following year.

There are many hotels, lodges, and camps that offer safari trips to visitors who want to see the animals on the Mara. Safaris are a good way to see the animals up close in the wild. You travel in a jeep and can be hidden by the tall grasses. Then you stop the car and wait, and soon enough you will see many animals, especially from July to September, when the herds of wildebeest have crossed into Kenya.

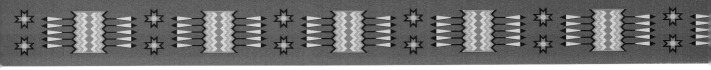

THE CATERPILLAR AND THE WILD ANIMALS

The Maasai live on Kenya's grassy plains together with various wild animals. This Maasai folktale tells of how the caterpillar can make even the elephant afraid.

ONCE there lived a hare whose house lay at the edge of the forest. Every day many animals passed by his house, and he was careful to lock his front door so that no one could wander in. One day he forgot to lock his door, and a caterpillar entered his home.

The hare returned and saw that his front door was open. He stood outside and said in a frightened voice, "Who has entered my house?"

The caterpillar replied in a loud voice, "It is I, the terrible wizard of the Mara. I can crush the mighty elephant and turn the rhinoceros into cow's dung!"

When the hare heard this, he grew terribly afraid. He went away, muttering, "What can a small hare like me do against such a powerful wizard?"

He went to ask the jackal for help to make the wizard go away. The jackal agreed, and they went to the hare's house.

Standing outside the front door, the jackal barked in a loud voice, "Who has entered the house of my friend, the hare?"

The caterpillar replied as before.

"What can I do against a wizard who can crush the mighty elephant?" asked the jackal and quickly slunk away.

The hare then asked the leopard to come and growl at the wizard. But the caterpillar answered in exactly the same way again, and the leopard went away too.

The hare asked the rhinoceros for help. The rhinoceros arrived at the hare's house, snorted and stomped his feet, and asked who had entered the hare's house. However, when he heard the reply, he said, "I don't want to be turned into cow's dung!" So away went the rhinoceros.

The poor hare could now only turn to the mighty elephant for help. The elephant came, blared his trumpet, and asked the question. Once again, the caterpillar gave the same reply.

"I am scared," said the elephant. "What can I do if this wizard crushes me?"

A frog passing by heard the shouting and offered to help. He went to the front door and asked, "Who has entered the

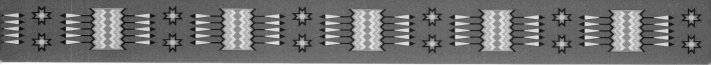

house of the hare?" The caterpillar replied in the same way.

Instead of going away, the frog crept closer to the door and croaked louder, "I am green and slimy and can leap up onto you and devour you in my large green mouth with my long green tongue!"

The caterpillar stopped eating and trembled. He saw the frog and squealed, "Please don't eat me, frog. I am only a little caterpillar."

The other animals who had gathered outside rushed in and dragged the caterpillar out. They laughed at the trouble he had caused, even the hare, who was so glad to have his house back.

E-MURATARE

The Samburu are an ethnic group that lives in central Kenya. E-muratare is the most important Samburu festival.

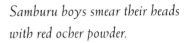

E-muratare takes place once every 14 years. It lasts for a year or more, culminating in Samburu boys becoming warriors, or *lmurran*.

The Samburu believe that *Ngai*, the supreme creator in their religion, lives close to mountain peaks, and they go there to ask for his blessings. They collect moss and herbs too.

The group returns to the elders, and the moss and herbs are roasted with a bull. This feast marks the beginning of *e-muratare*.

A few days later the boys gather and go from village to village singing and gathering more boys.

The families construct villages called *lorora*, where the ceremonies will take place. The boys and their families gather here, and the elders prepare the boys for their role as warriors. The next month there is feasting, and cattle are slaughtered to feed the boys. They are divided into groups, and each day some boys become warriors after some rituals are performed.

Warrior masks are a popular souvenir for visitors to Kenya.

Samburu boys smear their heads with red ocher powder.

First, they are blessed by the elders and go to a nearby stream to wash themselves. Later they return to the *lorora*.

The most important ceremony takes place here —the circumcision. Family members dance and sing, and some go into a trance.

The boys will become warriors a month later. There is laughter, dancing, and singing. The boys return to their mothers, who shave their heads.

They remove the black capes they have been wearing for months and put on white robes, which symbolize they are new warriors. They smear their heads with ocher, a red-colored paste, and wear colorful warrior jewelry.

A SAMBURU WARRIOR NECKLACE

YOU WILL NEED

Cardboard, reddish-brown in color
String of medium thickness
Medium-sized beads of various colors
Glue

Samburu men and women wear necklaces of colorful beads, large earrings, bangles, and rings. Warriors also paint their faces with ocher — a red-colored paste. They also smear ocher in their hair and braid their hair, which they never cut until they become elders.

1 Cut a strip of cardboard two inches wide and long enough to fit loosely around your neck. Punch two holes at each end of the strip.

2 Cut the string into pieces that are as long as the strip of cardboard. Take one piece of string, and tie a knot at one end.

3 Push through one color of bead followed by another. Alternate the beads until you reach the end of the string. Tie another knot.

4 Glue the string of beads to the top of the cardboard.

5 Repeat with another string. This time use two other colors of beads alternately. Glue this string of beads on the cardboard below the first string of beads

6 Create more strings of beads, and glue them onto the cardboard until the strip is completely covered.

7 When you have finished, let the glue dry. Tie a short piece of string to each of the holes at the end of the cardboard.

8 Wrap the necklace around your neck, and tie the two ends of string together.

JAMHURI DAY

Jamhuri Day falls on December 12 and marks the day that Kenya became fully independent from the British in 1963.

Kenyans are reminded of their non-independent past and celebrate their unity on December 12.

During Jamhuri Day children are reminded of how the founding father Jomo Kenyatta fought for independence. He became the first prime minister and was president of Kenya until his death in 1978. The children recall how their forefathers fought to keep their land and for better wages, medical facilities, and education.

Jamhuri Day is a public holiday, so schools and offices are closed. As you walk down the streets, you see the Kenyan flag on flagpoles. Shops also hang banners in the black, green, and red colors of the flag on the front of buildings.

On Jamhuri Day families spend the morning at a local stadium. The day begins with the singing of the National Anthem. The people are entertained with parades and speeches.

The parades are made up of marching bands and displays from the army, navy, and air force. In Nairobi the president inspects the guard of honor mounted by the armed forces. This is followed by comedy shows and patriotic songs and poems sung in praise of the achievements of Kenya's forefathers.

The celebrations are most elaborate in Nairobi. A highlight is the fly-by.

In olden times the people of Kenya worked hard to ensure a better life for their families.

Jet planes from the Kenya Air Force zoom past overhead leaving three trails of smoke in black, green, and red, the colors of the Kenyan flag.

The president then makes a moving speech to remind the people of how their forefathers fought hard and died to become independent. He encourages the people to remain loyal and patriotic to their country and live by the country's motto of *"Peace, Love, and Unity."*

The president advises the young people to study hard so one day they can become the leaders of the nation.

The president awards the "Elder of the Golden Heart" award on this day to people who have made outstanding contributions to the community or government service. The celebrations in Nairobi are shown live on television.

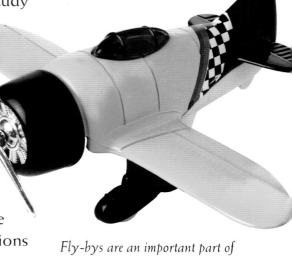

Fly-bys are an important part of Jamhuri Day celebrations.

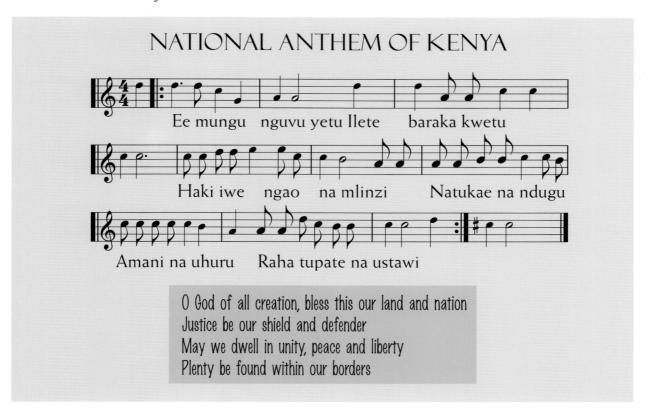

NATIONAL ANTHEM OF KENYA

Ee mungu   nguvu yetu Ilete   baraka kwetu

Haki iwe   ngao   na mlinzi   Natukae na ndugu

Amani na uhuru   Raha tupate na ustawi

O God of all creation, bless this our land and nation
Justice be our shield and defender
May we dwell in unity, peace and liberty
Plenty be found within our borders

HOW GOD GAVE CATTLE TO THE MAASAI

The Maasai believe that all cattle belong to them, since they were given to them by God himself. This is the story of how that happened.

WHEN God came to make the world, he found three things living together — a man from the Dorobo tribe, a serpent, and an elephant. One day the Dorobo man got a cow.

The Dorobo asked the serpent, "Why is it, whenever you breathe on me, I start to itch?" The serpent replied, "Father, I do not blow my bad breath on you on purpose." But the Dorobo did not believe the serpent and killed it with a club.

The elephant asked the Dorobo, "Where is the thin one?" The Dorobo looked away slyly and replied that he did not know. But the elephant was wiser than him and knew he was lying.

When the rains came, the Dorobo took his cow to the grasslands to graze and drink from puddles. In the meantime the elephant gave birth to a young one. By this time all the puddles had become dry, except for one.

The elephant went with her young to graze on the grasslands and wallow in the puddle. The Dorobo found the puddle muddy whenever he brought his cow to drink. This made him angry, and he picked up his arrow and killed the elephant.

The elephant calf was too frightened to stay with the evil Dorobo, so he ran away. The calf became friends with a Maasai and told him his story. The Maasai asked the elephant to take him to the Dorobo's home. They walked until they reached the hut, which God had turned upside down, with the door now turned to the sky.

God then called the Dorobo and said, "Come to me tomorrow morning, as I have something to tell you." The Maasai overheard this, and the next morning he went to God. He said to God, "I have come." God told him to take an axe and build a big house in three days. When it was ready, he was to search for a thin calf in the forest. He should bring the calf back to the house and slaughter it. The meat would be tied up in the hide and not eaten. The hide was to be fastened outside the door of the hut, firewood was to be fetched and a big fire lit, into which the meat would be thrown. He was then to stay in the hut and not be startled by the great noise outside.

The Maasai did as he was told, then entered the hut and left the fire burning.

God then sent a strip of hide down from heaven to where the calfskin hung. Cattle began to come down, until the whole corral was filled. The animals started pushing against one another until they began to break down the hut where the Maasai was hiding.

The Maasai was startled and uttered an exclamation of astonishment. He went outside and saw that the strip of hide was now cut, and no more cattle would come down. God said to the Maasai that this was all the cattle he would receive since he was warned not to be surprised.

The Maasai went away with his newly acquired cattle and took great care of them. The Dorobo lost the cattle and has had to shoot game for his food ever since.

MAULIDI ON LAMU

Maulidi is the Kenyan name for the Muslim festival celebrating the birth of the Prophet Muhammad, the founder of Islam. The most colorful celebrations are held on Lamu, an island that lies just off Kenya's Indian Ocean coast.

Maulidi on Lamu Island is held in June, during the third month of the Muslim calendar. The festival not only celebrates the birth of the Prophet Muhammad, who was born around 570 A.D., but also brings the people of Lamu Island together as a community. Many Muslim Kenyans from other parts of Kenya – as well as overseas tourists – visit Lamu during Maulidi celebrations.

Maulidi lasts for several days. The main festivities take place at the Riyadha Mosque, the main mosque on Lamu Island. On the eve of Maulidi the people of Lamu gather at the mosque to pray and sing. The mosque is lighted up and is a beautiful sight.

The people pray and sing until dawn. Later in the day groups of men perform traditional dances in the square in front of the mosque. Musicians playing hand-held drums accompany the dancers.

The dancers hold long walking sticks called *bakora*. They may also wield traditional curved Arab swords and stage pretend fights as part of the dancing. The dancing goes on for a few days.

On the last day of Maulidi groups of men and boys gather for a procession that winds itself through the main town

Flowers play an important role in any celebration, and at Maulidi they are used to decorate the home.

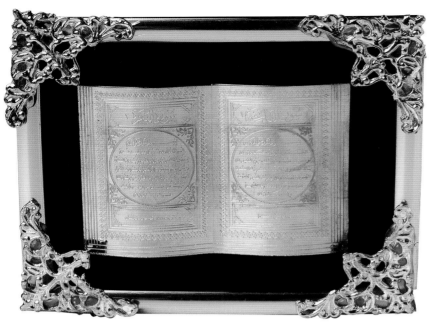

Muslims follow the teachings that are laid down in the Koran, Islam's holy book.

and along the coast. They link arms and walk down streets that are lined with crowds, who also sing and dance with them. It is a joyous and festive occasion.

Another highlight of Maulidi is the traditional donkey race that takes place along the seafront. Large crowds gather to watch the jockeys race their donkeys. The race is very fun to watch since some donkeys simply do not go where their riders want them to. Other donkeys throw off their riders or move so slowly, while others refuse to move at all!

The dhow race is also held as part of the festival. A dhow is a traditional Arab trading vessel with a tall, white, triangular sail. Spectators line the piers, jetties, and beaches of Lamu to see these dhows race with each other.

Other sports that are organized on Lamu during Maulidi include soccer, swimming, and running competitions.

Maulidi is a time to maintain the cultural traditions that are important to the people of Lamu. There are competitions to see who can best recite the Koran, Islam's holy book. Young children also take part in this recitation competition, and they memorize long passages from the Koran!

Other traditional activities include recitals of Swahili poetry and henna painting. Henna is a dye made from the henna plant and is used to decorate the hands and feet of Muslim brides in some parts of the Islamic world.

Tubes of henna are used to decorate the hands and feet of Muslim women.

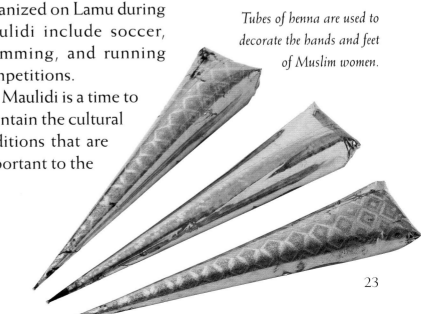

23

A KIKUYU WEDDING

The Kikuyu are a major ethnic group in Kenya. Most Kikuyu are Christian, although they still hold firm to their traditional beliefs. Their celebrations are a mixture of Christian rituals and ancient traditions.

Kikuyu weddings are seen as not only the union of the bride and groom, but also the union of the two families. Before the wedding there is an exchange of cattle and property from the groom's family to the bride's family.

Both families have to be in agreement as to how many possessions will be exchanged. A reasonable number of cattle are given to the groom's father-in-law. Sometimes goats are given instead, with ten goats equaling one cow.

It is also tradition for the groom to give gifts to the mother and father of the bride (*muhiki*). These vary from family to family but traditionally consist of a *mukwa* (head strap), *kiondo* (basket), *nguo ya maribe* (woman's dress made of skin and beads) for the mother and *ruhiu* (small sword), *itimu ria nduthu* (special spear) and *githii gia ikami* (man's cloak made of skin). Today the groom will give money instead of these items if that is what his in-laws prefer.

The main wedding ceremony takes place in a church, since most Kikuyu are Christians. There is singing and dancing of traditional wedding songs as the couple enters the

Gifts exchanged between the two families may include specially woven baskets.

church. The wedding party is made up of grooms, bridesmaids, flower girls, and pageboys, all dressed alike. After the service and exchange of rings the families go to the reception parties.

The first is held at the bride's house. It is tradition that the women of the bride's family prevent the groom from entering because they are sad that the bride is leaving their home. Often their sorrow can only be consoled with a "bribe." It is common to see hundreds of women barring the way for the groom while dancing. The bribe is collected in a basket, and the women let the groom enter. After cutting the cake and having some food and drink, the party moves on to the groom's home for further merrymaking.

Kikuyu weddings are a celebration for everyone in the village, who take part in the preparations.

IRIO

This is a traditional dish from central Kenya.

YOU WILL NEED

4 corn cobs
3/4 lb beans
4 potatoes
1 lb spinach or pumpkin leaves
Salt and pepper to taste
Saucepan

1 Boil the corn in a saucepan.

2 Remove from saucepan, and cut the kernels off the cobs.

3 Boil the beans in the saucepan until soft. Remove from saucepan.

4 Peel and wash the potatoes, and boil in saucepan.

5 Add corn, beans, and chopped spinach. Boil together until the potatoes are soft.

6 Season with salt and pepper, and mash.

7 Serve hot as an accompaniment to any meat dish.

MARALAL CAMEL DERBY

Have you ever heard of camel racing? Maralal is a town in central Kenya where the world's largest and most famous camel race takes place each year.

Camel races are extremely fun to watch, especially if the camels misbehave while racing.

The Maralal Camel Derby is Africa's best-known camel race. It takes place over one weekend in July or August in the town of Maralal and attracts local and overseas competitors.

Lots of Kenyans and tourists gather in Maralal to watch the races and experience the excitement of this unique festival. What makes the event more exciting is that the local Samburu people are out in force during the festival, and the streets of Maralal are filled with camels, Samburu warriors, and hundreds of visitors.

There are three main camel races during the derby—the amateur race, the semi-professional race, and the professional race. For the racers all you have to do is

For a better view of the races, the use of a pair of binoculars is advised.

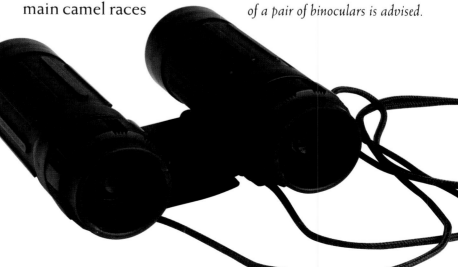

turn up, register for the event, pay some money, and choose your camel. The amateur race is 10 kilometers long, and you are allowed to hire a camel handler who will run behind your camel and keep your camel running by hitting it with a stick.

The semiprofessional race is 30 kilometers long, and you are also allowed a camel handler.

The professional race, at 42 kilometers, is the longest. In this race you are not allowed a camel handler. The world's best camel racers enter the professional race, and the winner gets a lot of money.

Sitting on a racing camel is uncomfortable since the animal moves in a lurching manner, and your body gets thrown back and forth. But there is nothing quite like racing a camel and feeling the desert breeze in your hair.

The most exciting moment in the races is the start. Many camels line up behind the start line, snorting and jostling each other. There is chaos as the racers are waved off. Some

The sun's bright rays may cause difficulty in watching the races, so most spectators wear sunglasses.

camels bolt ahead, while others run in the wrong direction. Many camels refuse to budge, while some walk slowly, ignoring the beating from the camel handler.

There are also cycling races that use mountain bikes. Children join in the racing during the donkey races. The donkeys are gentler than camels but can be just as stubborn!

There are other events such as dancing and musical performances, showcasing Kenya's many ethnic groups and cultures.

Because of the heat umbrellas are used to shield the crowd from the sun.

27

A Tie-Dye T-shirt

It is quite warm in Maralal during the camel derby, and you should wear light clothes if you visit during this time. How about a tie-dye T-shirt? It's easy to make and will keep you cool. This style is popular with young Kenyans. Best of all, your shirts are really colorful after you dye them.

YOU WILL NEED

Different colored dyes, such as light
blue, dark blue, and purple, in
plastic bottles
An old T-shirt, preferably white
6 thick rubber bands
Gloves
Old newspapers

1 Lay the old newspapers on your work surface to keep the dye from staining the surface. Put down several layers.

2 Place the T-shirt flat, and fold the shirt in half by putting one sleeve onto the other sleeve. Fold in half again. Then fold it one more time. Your shirt should now be folded into a long strip of about 4 to 6 inches width.

3 Take one end of the shirt in your left hand and the other in your right hand, and twist the shirt in opposite directions, making several turns.

4 Take a rubber band, and tie it around one end of the shirt.

5 Tie the remaining rubber bands along the shirt, leaving about 3 inches between each rubber band. The shirt is now divided into 6 or 7 sections by the rubber bands.

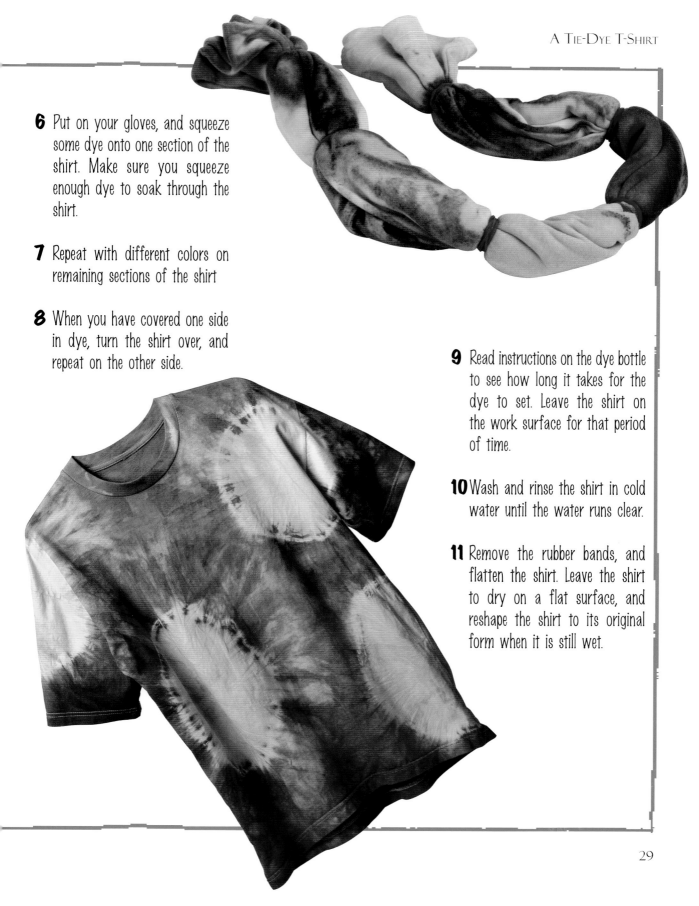

6 Put on your gloves, and squeeze some dye onto one section of the shirt. Make sure you squeeze enough dye to soak through the shirt.

7 Repeat with different colors on remaining sections of the shirt

8 When you have covered one side in dye, turn the shirt over, and repeat on the other side.

9 Read instructions on the dye bottle to see how long it takes for the dye to set. Leave the shirt on the work surface for that period of time.

10 Wash and rinse the shirt in cold water until the water runs clear.

11 Remove the rubber bands, and flatten the shirt. Leave the shirt to dry on a flat surface, and reshape the shirt to its original form when it is still wet.

Diwali

Kenya has a significant minority of Asian Indians who live in Nairobi, Mombasa, Kisumu, and Nakuru. Most of them are Hindus, and the main Hindu festival is Diwali, the Festival of Lights, which falls in late October or early November.

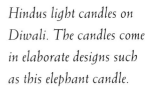

Diwali, also called the Hindu New Year, is a time of renewal and signifies the victory of good over evil. It celebrates a traditional Hindu story from the epic Ramayana, an ancient Indian book. Hindus also believe that Diwali is a time when Lakshmi, the Goddess of Wealth, visits their homes and leaves her blessings.

Preparation for Diwali takes place weeks before the festival. Homes and businesses are cleaned. Parents buy gifts for their children. People shop for new clothes. Women start preparing special Diwali sweets. Some families also prepare rangolis in front of their houses. They are decorative patterns made of rice flour and different colored dye powder.

The festival lasts for several days. People don their new clothes and visit friends and relatives. Children receive gifts and eat lots of delicious sweets. Kenyans celebrate Diwali at parties in the home and in Hindu temples.

One of the most magical scenes of Diwali is

Hindus light candles on Diwali. The candles come in elaborate designs such as this elephant candle.

the hundreds of tiny lamps that are placed around and outside the homes of Hindu families in Nairobi. These lights signify the triumph of light over darkness. Diwali is a great time for children, since they wear new clothes, eat tasty sweets, and receive presents from their parents and relatives.

Words to Know

Circumcision: The act of cutting off the skin at the tip of the male sex organ.

Coincides: To happen at the same time or during the same period.

Culminating: To reach the highest point or highest development.

Epic: A long poem that tells the story of the deeds of gods and great men and women.

Ethnic: Of a racial, national, or tribal group.

Hide: An animal's skin.

Jostling: To bump or push against in a rough manner.

Lurching: To move with irregular swinging or rolling movements.

Maasai: The native people of South Kenya.

Migration: The act of traveling regularly from one part of the world to another, according to the seasons of the year.

Pastures: Grassy land where farm animals feed.

Rituals: One or more ceremonies or customary acts, which are often repeated in the same form.

Safari: A trip through wild country, especially in east or central Africa, hunting or photographing wild animals.

Slaughtered: To kill an animal for meat or food.

Smear: To cause something to spread across a surface.

Snorting: To make a rough noise by forcing air down the nose.

Vessel: A ship or a large boat.

Wield: To have or use.

ACKNOWLEDGMENTS

WITH THANKS TO:
Eric Koh, Selina Kuo, Lydia Leong, Yumi Ng, Daphne Rodrigues, and Alan Tay for the loan of artifacts.

PHOTOGRAPHS BY:
Haga Library, Japan (cover), Yu Hui Ying (all other pictures).

ILLUSTRATIONS BY:
Amy Ong (p. 1, p. 7), Enrico Sallustio (pp. 4-5), Lee Kowling (p. 15), and Ong Lay Keng (p. 21).

SET CONTENTS